Lazzette Ohman

Reflections:
A Pioneer Alaskan's Personal History from the Gold Rush of '89 to 1980

Lazzette M. Ohman

VANTAGE PRESS
New York / Los Angeles / Chicago

To my loving family, Gunnar Ohman, my husband, and my daughter, Lauren Shelley, and son, Gerald "Jerry" Shelley

FIRST EDITION

Published by Vantage Press, Inc.
516 West 34th Street, New York, New York 10001

Manufactured in the United States of America
ISBN: 0-533-07795-8

Library of Congress Catalog Card No.: 87-91826

Contents

Author's Note

In the back of my mind I have always wanted to write and tell the public in words how my life was as a child in comparison to today. After I had lived in Funter Bay for twenty one years, I really wanted to tell a few of my stories and experiences being married to Gunnar, an outdoorsman and lover of life. I dedicate this story to Gunnar. How many people would pay for just a day, week, or a month? I had twenty-one years.

Acknowledgments

For the generous help, cooperation in guiding me and giving me encouragement to put down my experiences and memories, I sincerely thank the following: My family, Gunnar, Jerry, and Lauren, who have been so patient and helpful; Connie Davis, who gave me my first instructions on how to start; Leisa Wilson, for her inspiration on how to "let out" my experiences, as I am a very private person; Carol Mogensen, for editing and putting together in concise form; Pat Walsh, for the photo of Gunnar and myself.

Introduction

Gold lured my grandfather to Alaska. Lewis Wilkes (he preferred being called L.C.) arrived in Skagway in 1898 along with thousands of other men and women whom he described as having a vision of gold and fortune that carried them through unimaginable hardships and dangers. Grandfather Wilkes actually settled at Dyea, which was a short distance from Skagway. My grandmother, Jessie Esther, and their infant daughter, Marvel (my mother) left Nebraska that same year to join him. Today Dyea is a ghost town, but in 1898 there were about thirty thousand people living there—mostly in tents. Few of them planned to stay permanently; it was just a temporary stopover where the miners outfitted themselves before crossing the Chilkoot Pass on the way to the gold in the Yukon. My grandfather's brother was already in the freight business in Dyea and convinced L.C. that there was more money in supplying the "stampeders" than there was in prospecting. So, L.C. invested his savings in horses and became a freight packer.

When the freight arrived at Dyea, it was stored in the Wilkes and Vining warehouse until the miners could pick it up. From Dyea it had to be packed to the Scales, which was the last base before the final climb to the Summit and the beginning of the Chilkoot Pass. This was as far as freight could be carried by animals. From the Scales the miners had to pack their supplies on their backs up a forty-five degree incline to the Summit, a distance of only two thousand feet, but the part of the trip that the miners dreaded most. L.C. loaded his horses at Dyea and charged sixteen cents a pound to take freight from there to the Scales. From the Scales to the Summit the freighters had to carry everything on their backs, and the charge for that grueling work was one dollar a pound.

Some of my grandfather's memoirs of those wild and exciting days were published in an article that appeared in the June 1948 issue of the *Alaska Sportsman* magazine. In that article L.C. tells of the gold rushers who couldn't afford a packer to take their freight and used everything from hand sleds to goats. He told about one fellow who brought two steers, thinking he'd have fresh beefsteaks to butcher when he arrived in the Klondike; however, he couldn't haul enough food to feed the steers, let alone haul his own freight. Another man used goats and had better luck. Three of the goats, harnessed and hooked tandem, could haul a fair load on a smooth trail. Unfortunately, the sled dogs thought the goats were fair game and ate them— everything but the horns and harnesses.

The two prize cargoes in those days, according to my grandfather, were silk and whiskey—"silk for the dance hall girls and whiskey for the multitude." The silk could be safely transported anywhere in the interior in soldered waterproof tin boxes packed in stout wooden crates. American whiskey was cheaper than Canadian, but there was also a high duty on it. To avoid paying the duty, packers had to use more ingenious methods to get whiskey past Candian customs. The most successful method was to hide a pony keg or bottles in the middle of bales of hay.

The freight business was short-lived. Most of the miners crossed the Dyea Trail during the first five months of 1889 when the rivers were frozen and the ice and snow made sledding easy. L.C. read the writing on the wall and got out of the freight packing business when a company installed a steam-powered tram to the Summit. Eventually the tram lowered their freight rate to the Summit to only two and a half cents a pound. During these years, Grandmother also added to the family income by baking and selling bread to the miners.

With the end of the freighting business, L.C. had to find another way of supporting his family, so he went to work laying ties for the White Pass–Yukon Railroad. My mother became the first white child to travel on that railroad when the company gave her a lifetime pass.

The forty thousand miners in Dyea folded up their tents and left as quickly as they arrived. My grandfather was one of the last to leave, staying there, he said, "until the last dog was hung." When they finally left Dyea, L.C. and Jessie returned to Skagway, which prospered for several more years. They knew the infamous Soapy Smith personally; in fact, the day Soapy was shot, L.C. was standing on an adjacent dock. Grandfather continued working for the railroad, and until 1908, he, Jessie, and Marvel divided their time between Skagway, Valdez, Seward, Katalla, and Cordova. In 1908 they settled in Ketchikan. Most of the stories that I heard about the gold rush were told to me by my grandmother and mother. I only met my grandfather once because he and Jessie Esther divorced while my mother was still in her teens.

After the divorce Marvel stayed with her dad. She spent hours in his cabinet shop learning carpentry skills, and it was around the shop's potbellied stove that she heard many of the stories told by the men who were a part of the Alaska gold rush.

Grandmother married Harry Carroll, a cook who had come to Alaska from Boston. They left Ketchikan on the steamship *Jefferson* and moved to Juneau and bought the Brunswick Rooms. Later my grandmother and step-grandfather sold the rooming house and bought a small grocery store on Franklin Street, just south of the old Nugget Shop.

Reflections

Sukoi Island

In 1919, the year I was born, there was a terrible flu epidemic. So many people died that their bodies were stacked like cordwood on the street until they could be properly buried. It was also near the end of World War I, and every steamboat coming to Ketchikan carried soldiers returning home. My father, Milo C. Caughrean, worked as a chief diesel engineer on one of the Alaska steamships that made weekly trips between Seattle and Juneau. Milo was away from Ketchikan so much that this soon interfered with the marriage, so my parents divorced while Marvel was still in her early twenties. I stayed with my mother, and my older brother, Clifford, went to California with my father.

My first childhood memories are of Sukoi Iskand, which is a few miles southeast of Petersburg. I was only four years old when we went there to live after Mother married Tom Shearer, a Scot from the Orkney Islands. Tom tended a fox farm there for the owner. No one else lived on the island, and my only playmates were the blue foxes, which were allowed to run free. I played hide-and-seek with them, hiding behind stumps and in any hole I could find. Tom also raised silver foxes, but these were kept in pens. One of my earliest memories concerns one of the blue foxes and the first toy I remember getting. Mother and Tom had given me a toy pistol, and the first night Mother placed it on the windowsill near my bed. While I slept, one of the blue foxes stole the pistol. I remember looking everywhere on the island for that pistol and scolding every fox that I saw. Finally I found it hidden in one of the fox's dens.

1

Sometimes Mother and Tom took me in the skiff when they hunted hair seals, which they cooked up into a porridge for the foxes. I sat in the bottom of the skiff while Tom rowed and Marvel shot the seals and grabbed them before they sank. Mother was an excellent shot. Once she accepted a wager from some men who bet that she couldn't shoot an eagle out of a distant tree. (During this time the Alaska Territory paid $2.50 per pair of eagle claws.) She shot the eagle, and when it didn't fall the men claimed they had won the bet. Mother didn't give in to their banter. Even though she used crutches as the result of a surgical mishap several years earlier, she climbed the tree and found that someone had tied the dead eagle to it. Nobody was telling her she missed! Years later she was barred from joining the Juneau Rifle Club—no one could beat her.

Sukoi Island was joined to another smaller island by a handmade swinging bridge that had a rope for a handrail. Sometimes I went with Tom when he made his rounds of the two islands to feed the foxes. I remember that on the smaller island there were Indian graves scattered among the trees, many of them buried between tree roots. In those days there were fox farms all over southeast Alaska. (Some of those farms were fronts for lucrative moonshining operations.)

We left Sukoi Island in 1923. My brother Clifford had returned to live with us, and since he was ready to enter first grade, we had to live where he could go to school. We moved to Juneau, which was a big city to me. Marvel and Tom bought a place three and a half miles from town, near Salmon Creek, which had once been the residence of the superintendent for the Boston Mining Company. When we moved, it was the last house on the only road out of Juneau. A few years later a two-rut road was extended all the way to the Mendenhall Glacier.

Juneau 1921–41

We were really out in the country. The Juneau Dairy was located across the highway from the downtown cemetery, where Harborview School now stands. During the summer months, the dairy pastured their cattle at about Mile 9, where Fred Myers's store and Nugget Mall are located. We had very few neighbors at our new home. In the summer, Indian Jim and his family arrived at their fish camp at the mouth of Salmon Creek, and I became friends with Indian Jim's daughter, who was about my age. The two of us spent the summer exploring the woods or watching the elders catch fish and prepare them for smoking. A big event in my memory was the day I was invited to their potlatch, which was held in a big square building with a large bonfire built in a square in the center of the building. The elders sat around and talked in Tlingit, and even though I couldn't understand them and it was very dark in he room with the only light coming from the bonfire, I felt wonderful and excited. Mother had told me that it was something special to be invited to a potlatch!

One rainy day I decided to visit my new friend at their camp just across the stream from our house. The tide was getting high, and the only way I could cross the stream was to walk on a log that had been made slippery by rains. When I fell, Indian Jim pulled me from the water, gently shook me and said, "Now, little white one, you go home." At first I was confused and thought he didn't like me, but later realized that he only wanted me to hurry home and get dry. That was also the summer Mother got fish poison in her hand from cleaning all of the fresh salmon that Indian Jim had given her. Indian Jim told her to make a poultice for the infected cut by placing a piece of fresh salmon on it and wrapping it up. This she did, and it seemed to be working, but still Mother got worried and went into town to see a doctor.

Indian Jim taught Tom how to prepare bait from dog salmon eggs. It was good bait, as Tom was always able to catch the large amounts of fish that he needed to make porridge for the silver foxes he kept in pens.

My mother was a doer—whatever needed to be done, she found a way to tackle it. Not long after we moved into our house, she decided that it was too small and that Clifford and I needed rooms of our own. Mom drew up plans and put all of her carpentry skills to use. She was happy and having fun all the while. Several years later she added on a back porch and installed a food cooler and a sink in the floor where she could drain her wash water. She also built me a log cabin for a playhouse, complete with cupboard, table and chairs, and a child-size cast iron stove that I could actually use to heat the cabin or cook. I soon learned that when Marvel was working (especially if she hit her finger or missed a nail) there were words I wasn't to repeat. Boy, could she cuss!

Mother had quite a green thumb; our yard was full of all kinds of flowers. After the dirt road was extended to the Mendenhall Glacier, busloads of tourists would stop on their way back from the glacier to pick bouquets of flowers from our yard. They never made a dent in her garden.

When my mother was younger, she had surgery that left one of her legs paralyzed, and the doctor told her that she would have to use crutches the rest of her life. It took a near tragedy to make her realize that she could do without them. We were living on Sukoi Island, and I was playing outdoors near the house when I looked up and saw fire coming out of the roof. I ran inside and told Mother, who ran to the porch, grabbed her rifle, fired three shots to signal Tom to get home, then ran upstairs and rolled two large trunks containing her prized possessions downstairs and outside. It wasn't until the fire was put out that she realized she had been working without her crutches. With that realization, her leg buckled under her and she fell. After that, Mom was determined to walk again without crutches. Every day she worked at wiggling her toes and moving her ankle. In a matter of a few months she was able to throw away the crutches, and she never used them again. She was a determined, tough individual.

Since our house was at the end of the road, my stepdad applied for and got the contract to drive the school bus. One day he had to be out of town, leaving the bus driving to my mother. She was pretty scared. This was her first trip alone, and she had to pick up all the children from Salmon Creek on into Juneau. Mother managed to get all of the kids to school and back to their homes without incident, until she drove into the garage. That's when she forgot the brakes and drove through the back wall. Fortunately she was good with a hammer. With Clifford and me helping, she had the wall repaired before Tom returned the next day. Tom asked why all the sawdust was on the garage floor, but none of us admitted anything, and Tom never said any more about it. I think he had figured out what happened and just wanted us to know that the sawdust didn't go by unnoticed.

The Boston Mining Company operated until 1914. One of the owners, John Wagner, continued living at the mine and was one of our few neighbors. He was a frequent visitor at our house, and he never objected to having us kids hanging around him at the mine. As I recall, the mine consisted of one large building that contained the office, bunkhouse, kitchen, and storage. After the mine closed, John helped men who were having hard times by letting them stay at the mine and do odd jobs for room and board. John was one of two people who sticks in my mind for the charity work he did for others. The other was Mary Joyce, who came to Juneau much later and achieved a certain amount of fame throughout Alaska.

Sam and Mabel Jacobsen were friends of my parents who lived at Warm Springs Bay. Since there was no school at Warm Springs, they sent their son, Ray, who was two years older than Clifford, to live with us and attend school in Juneau. One day the three of us were poking around a woodshed near our house when the boys noticed that the boards joining the woodshed and the mink pens sounded hollow. A check of the back wall revealed that it also was hollow. Marvel pried one end of a large plank from the back wall and found a large empty space. This, she decided, was where bootleggers from the earlier years stored their booze until someone came by to pick up the supply.

We really got excited when Mother explained that the booze probably was brewed nearby. That's all we needed to hear to get us started on a search of the woods. Eventually, we found four different stills. Most of them were broken up, either by law officers or the bootleggers themselves because the law was onto them. Later we found two more stills near the mine, and sometimes I found a bottle or two of whiskey buried between the tree roots. Once Mother noticed a man standing at the end of the road watching our house. We later found out that he was the United States marshall, and we wondered if he suspected us of being involved in bootlegging, even though the stills were broken up before we discovered them.

Juneau was a big city to me in those days, but Douglas was even larger. I never once went there until the bridge was built in 1936, and then I was nearly grown. Before the bridge, the only way to get from Juneau to Douglas was by ferry. There was also a community of about two thousand living at the company's camp on Perseverance Trail. Later, during my teen years, my stepdad owned a tailor shop and took in dry cleaning for the camp, and I often made deliveries there. I enjoyed the walk and was always invited to stay for dinner. Today you read about how wild and rough the early gold mining days were, but I was never afraid to go to the camp alone and was always treated with respect; the miners not only liked me, they spoiled me. "One Arm Dick" was the handle of one the workers who made sure that I was well treated.

Tom's tailor shop was a favorite stop for fishermen and miners, who often invited him next door for a drink at the New York Tavern. Eventually, the drinking became a major problem, causing Mother to leave Tom several times during their marriage. When he was sober, Tom was a good man and a good father. When he drank he mistreated my mother. Once, after one of his drinking bouts, Mother and I moved out. I think it was during this time that Mom learned that she and Tom had not been legally married because she had not applied in California for her final divorce papers from my real father.

We had barely got our things moved into the newly built Johnson Apartments on Gastineau Avenue when Mother got a letter that made her fume. I sat among the unpacked trunks and boxes while Mom read the letter. Between the cussing and fuming I finally learned that the letter was from my real father, announcing that he would arrive that evening on the Alaska steamship with the apparent intention of moving in with us. Mom told me to stay put and not let anyone inside the apartment. Then she left, saying that there wasn't anyway he was going to move in after neglecting his family all of these years. Marvel wasn't gone long, but when she returned it seemed pretty obvious that she had settled the problem once and for all. We soon returned to live with Tom at the Salmon Creek house.

My teen years in high school were spent in much the same way high school students spend their time today. I worked on the high school newspaper, the *J-Bird* (it still goes by that name), and had to learn lines from Shakespeare. Mother said that "for someone being dead for four hundred years, he was still a pain!" As a teen, I was allowed to attend more events in town, such as dances at the Moose lodge. The big events were Memorial Day, the Fourth of July, and Labor Day. For these occasions many of the local organizations had elaborate picnics near our place at Salmon Creek. The men built shelves between the trees: one for soda pop, one for beer, one for boxes of candy bars, pastries, or other desserts. There were also big containers of all kinds of ice cream. The meat, roast pig or beef, usually was cooked in large pits. Because we lived close by, Clifford and I always got acqainted with the men preparing the picnic area, and we were always invited. No one had a lot of money in those days, but it seemed that people were always able to get together for a big party.

Every August Juneau held the Southeast Alaska Fair in a large corrugated iron building on Willoughby Avenue where the Bill Ray Center is located. When I was fourteen I won first place for a needlework entry! Tom usually came home with a silver trophy for his silver foxes. My grandmother was the "caller" for the spinning wheel game, which meant calling out the numbers that were pinned to the wheel.

Tom had a beautiful singing voice and was often asked to entertain at the lodge parties. I was so proud of his voice and loved singing the Scottish ballads with him as we drove home. You could always tell when Tom had too many drinks at one of those parties because the more he drank, the slower he drove. But, because of his continued drinking, my teens were becoming more unsettled and insecure.

Two people who helped me through this time were Walter and Ethel Bendseil. Walter rented space in Dad's tailor shop to run his transfer business. Whenever Dad was drinking and ornery, Marvel had me stay with Ethel and Walter. I wasn't the only young person the Bendseils helped; their door was always open to young people. Tom's drinking became worse during my teens and finally contributed to his death in 1937, not long after I graduated from high school.

These were confusing and sad times for me, and I was very happy to meet Harry Peterson, who was fun, kind, and polite. I became pregnant, and when I told Mother, she demanded that I move out. I moved in with my brother and his new bride. Gerald was born on November 16, 1938, and Mother asked me to return home. I found a clerking job at Jim Ellen's grocery store and divided my time between working and taking care of "Jerry."

It was during one of my stays with the Bendseils that I met Robert "Happy" Shelley, who worked as a cook on the forest service boat, *Ranger VIII*. Whenever he was in town, he would come by in the evenings for a visit and game of pinochle with Ethel and Walter. The rest of the time he was building a home on Peterson Hill near Auke Lake. Happy asked me to marry him, and I thought this would be best and would give me more time with Jerry. We married on March 14, 1941. Happy's forest service job ended, so he decided to look for work in Anchorage. Hitler was stirring things up in Europe at that time, and Anchorage was beginning to enjoy a boom that continued through World War II and for several more years.

Juneau did not change much between 1921 and 1941, but it certainly looks different today. Exceptionally high tides almost reached Willoughby Avenue, and all the houses from Seventh Street up to Eleventh Street were built on pilings because the incoming tide came up to the plank sidewalks. A friend of mine lived on Eighth Street, and I can remember her mother sweeping water out of the house after an exceptionally high tide. Over the years, Willoughby and the area along the waterfront were filled with rock and gravel taken from the Alaska-Juneau Mine.

Events and people that made a strong impression on me during those years include Mary Joyce, a young nurse who came to Juneau from Wisconsin and accepted a job caring for Hackley Smith. Hackley was a wealthy eccentric alcoholic who was the son of L.C. Smith, founder of the typewriter company. His family bought a homestead for him up the Taku River, had a cabin built, and arranged for Mary Joyce to be his private nurse.

Mary brought Hackley to Juneau only about two times a year and always stopped at Dad's shop to leave clothes to be cleaned. I liked Mary right away; she was a wisp of a person with jet black, short bobbed hair and the prettiest blue eyes and fair skin. When Hackley entered the shop, Dad would tell me to go to the back room, which I gladly did because Smith was always drunk, loud, and vulgar. Mary inherited the homestead after Hackley died in 1932.

In 1935 she became somewhat of a celebrity when she set out to fulfill a dream to drive a five-dog team to Fairbanks. She began her trip December 20, accompanied by an Indian guide and his two sons, who would accompany her as far as Atlin. From there she intended to travel alone. It wasn't easy crossing the fast, cold running water that flowed between the icy banks of the Taku River. At one point she crossed on her hands and knees while her dogs crossed over on boughs placed atop poles that the Indians laid over the gaps in the ice.

Mary reached Atlin January 7, then headed for Carcross alone, en route to Whitehorse. I remember hearing on the radio that she arrived at Tanana Crossing in March in time to fly to Fairbanks for the Ice Carnival. It took her about three months to travel by dogsled from the Taku River to Fairbanks. She flew back to her homestead, which today is owned by Ron Moss and serves as a lodge for tourists and visitors from Juneau.

Mary Joyce later moved to town and opened a bar and liquor store in the old Alaskan Hotel. She also owned some small cabins where anyone who was down and out could spend a comfortable night. Juneau was her home until she died in 1979.

Someone else I remember, although I never met her, was the little girl who became trapped in a mudslide November 21,1936. She was buried for hours under a bathtub that had turned over and covered her. A pipe from the tub protruded through the mud, giving her some air. Rescuers rushed her to St. Ann's Hospital, but she died three hours later.

The slide roared down Mount Roberts at 7:30 P.M., taking in its path four houses and leaving a pile of debris that was twenty feet deep and seventy-five feet wide. Most of the buildings that were swept away were apartments. Ten families lived in the Nickinovich Apartments. The slide also caught the Matson Boarding House, the Hugo Peterson Building, and the Gus Erickson residence. Fourteen people were killed outright. Power and telephone lines were torn out, leaving the city in total darkness, and the coast guard cutter *Tallapoosa* and an army launch *Fornance* lit the scene with floodlights.

It was also in 1936 when fire destroyed the Coliseum Theatre and apartments above the theater. The fire didn't destroy the impressive pipe organ that had been installed in the theater in 1928 as accompaniment for silent movies. In 1939 when W. D. Gross opened his new theater on Front Street, he had the organ stored in the 20th Century Building. The organ was later sold to Letha and Miles Remly, who donated it to the state in 1975. Through public donations, the organ was restored and permanently installed on the eighth floor of the State Office Building.

A more devastating fire started in the rear of the Douglas Cash Grocery Store early one winter morning in 1937. A high north wind fanned the flames, spreading flying embers to other businesses, until the entire business section of Douglas was wiped out. Killing the fire was out of the question, so firemen concentrated their efforts on keeping the fire within as small an area as possible. The fire spread in two directions from its source, traveling along the water side of Front Street before being driven toward town by the wind, encircling the commercial district. Volunteer firemen from Douglas and Juneau saved at least a dozen homes. Luckily, the Juneau-Douglas Bridge had been finished the previous year. The Salvation Army and the Red Cross contributed to help those who lost their homes, and residents from both Juneau and Douglas opened their doors and purses to help. Juneau and Douglas have always been staunch rivals, but during this time the two communities became "family" working together.

I remember the thrill of the arrival of the Alaska Steamship's boat just before Christmas and how it was lit up and decorated. Bright lights and a large Christmas tree lit up the inside. The townspeople were invited aboard, and Santa Claus was there passing out stockings full of candy to the children as they left the boat.

It was during this period that Patsy Ann, a stone deaf English pit terrier, met every steamship that came into Juneau. No one seemed to know where she came from or whether anyone had ever claimed her as a pet. She belonged to no one and everyone. Patsy Ann had an uncanny knowledge of the Alaska Steamship schedule. No matter where she was or what she was doing, minutes before the boat arrived, Patsy Ann headed for the dock and was always there awaiting its arrival.

Patsy Ann became Juneau's official greeter in a ceremony conducted by the mayor and attended by the City Council, city magistrate, and representatives of the Commonwealth. After being shampooed and pedicured for the occasion, this homely old dog was presented with a gold plated collar bearing the engraved inscription, "Official Greeter, Patsy Ann," and a shiny new brass tag that entitled her to appear in public anywhere within the environs of the city.

Anchorage

Gerald and I left Juneau in July 1941 on the Alaskan steamship *Yukon* for Seward, enroute to Anchorage. Friends of ours in Juneau, Milton and Betty Ward, were also relocating to Anchorage. Milton was already there, so Betty traveled with us. I left Juneau ahead of Happy so that I could make a trip to Flat and get acquainted with my real father.

At Seward we boarded the Alaska Railroad Company's train for the trip to Anchorage. It was my first train ride and the scenery was spectacular, but rounding constant curves and traveling across trestles at unbelievably high elevations made me extremely nervous. After rounding one of the curves, we got our first glimpse of Anchorage in the distance, and what a disappointment! There didn't seem to be many buildings, and what there were appeared to be warehouses. I soon realized that we had only seen the railroad yard. I was relieved to see that Anchorage did have stores along Fourth Avenue (which was the main street) and hotels scattered here and there. World War II had turned Anchorage, which previously had been a supply base for the railroad, into a boom town. Elmendorf Air Force Base and Fort Richardson were being built, and jobs were plentiful.

Milton met us at the depot and took us to his and Betty's new home. Like most of the new settlers in Anchorage, he had bought a lot and set up a tent until he could build something more permanent. Milton told me that the lot next to theirs was for sale and suggested that we buy it once Happy arrived from Juneau.

The next morning I bought tickets for passage on a Star Airlines plane, and Gerald and I left for a visit with my father in Flat. Flat, located on Otter Creek about seven miles east of the Iditarod River, had once been a busy placer mining community; however, by 1941 most of the miners had left to join the war effort and only a few private claims were being worked. My father and his partner had a small placer mine on Black Creek.

In 1931 there were 124 people living at Flat, and by 1941 there probably were only half that many. Alaska Communication Service had a station operated by one man who kept the community informed of world news, but few people had radios and reception was terrible. There was a grocery store, an assayer's office, and a few abandoned buildings. One of our side trips was to drive to Iditarod, which was only three and a half miles from Flat. Iditarod, the supply and commercial center of the Innoke-Iditarod Placer Mining District, had dwindled from a population of seven hundred in 1931 to one lonely soul in 1941. When it had been the commercial hub of the area, it contained many stores and a large bank. Now all that was left of the bank was the cement vault. My father told me that the ground around the vault had been well sifted for any gold dust thay may have fallen through the planked floor.

After a month's visit, Gerald and I returned to Anchorage and found that Happy had arrived, bought the lot next to Milton and Betty, and put up a sixteen-by-twenty celotex home. It was a rush job, but well done. I picked moss and dried it to use as insulation around the windows and under the subfloor. Soon we had shelves, partitions, and a coal-burning stove. Years later, when street markers were added, our home officially was located at Fifteenth and F streets.

Actually, by the standards of the day our house was pretty comfortable. Most people were still living in tents or eight-by-ten buildings. It wasn't uncommon to see large engine crates covered with tar paper and a smokestack protruding from the top. Housing was so scarce that in some areas it wasn't safe to leave your "home" unoccupied. There were occasions when someone would drive a truck up to one of the small buildings, pick it up and move it to another lot. The thieves then hurridly repainted the building. People were so busy coming and going, surrounded by trucks hauling building materials, that nobody gave it a thought. Imagine coming home from work and finding an empty lot!

Rick and Vanola Richards, whom I had met in Juneau, were especially good friends of mine during the years I lived in Anchorage. I first met them in 1933 when they were living in a small cabin about one mile from Juneau. This cabin must have caused them a little embarrassment because as long as it was there, it was known as the "pest house," a nickname that it earned when it served as the hospital's quarantine house.

When we first arrived in Anchorage, Rick and Vanola were operating an electrical business. Rick was also a licensed surveyor and later he and Vanola obtained pilots' licenses and flew all over the north conducting mineral surveys. Later Vanola had the distinction of being the only woman licensed by the Canadian government to conduct airborne mineral surveys in the Canadian Artic.

It seemed that everyone in Anchorage had jobs related to the war effort. In January 1943 I went to work for the Alaska Air Depot under the War Department. I got up very early and walked fourteen blocks by moonlight to catch the morning bus that took me to Elmendorf Air Depot, and at night walked home by moonlight. During those short winter months, I never saw daylight on the days that I worked. All the windows at work were blacked out to

evenings at the Southside Grocery, and Happy picked up carpentry jobs. But the marital problems continued. Soon Lauren became ill, and the doctor said that she was susceptible to tuberculosis and should be taken south to a warmer climate.

By now we owned five lots, but only put the house and one lot up for sale. We sold the house and lot for fourteen thousand dollars, which seemed a good return, as we only paid three hundred for each lot. We loaded our pickup to the hilt and prepared for the long drive to Monterey, California. Gerald was enrolled in Mount Lowe Military Academy, which turned out to be a good choice. He and Happy had never been close; Happy just never seemed to be able to accept him as his son. Happy and I stayed together until our divorce in 1952.

After the divorce, I received a letter from Gunnar Ohman, whom I had known in Juneau during the early forties. Gunnar had been a good companion during the unsettled years before I met Happy. He was a nice person to be with, full of humor and good clean fun. He had been engaged to a girl from his hometown of Boras, Sweden, and eventually returned to Sweden with the intention of marrying her. He soon learned that she had changed her mind about leaving Sweden and resettling in the Alaska wilderness.

We corresponded for a while, and one day I received a box of assorted canned goods that Gunnar had put up himself—venison, fish, clams. I swallowed the bait hook, line, and sinker. In 1957 I took Lauren and visited my mother in Ballard, Wahington, for Christmas and invited Gunnar to join us there. After Christmas Gunnar returned with us to Monterey, and we were married January 25. In May I returned to Alaska and a new life at Gunnar's homestead in Funter Bay.

Funter Bay

Gunnar arrived in New York from Sweden in 1928. He spent his first two years in Chicago working, but city life was not his dream. He wanted to go to Alaska where he hoped he could earn a living by fishing and trapping. Gunnar had been told about an uncle that went to Alaska during the gold rush of 1889, and he hoped to find him, although the family assumed that the uncle was dead.

In Chicago Gunnar met another young Swede, Ragner Berg, and the two traveled to Seattle where they purchased steerage tickets on a steamship for Ketchikan. Both were young and strong. Gunnar had a beautiful singing voice and a sense of humor that made him the life of any gathering. Ragnar was more reserved with a dry sense of humor. At first the two worked as part of a road construction crew until they had enough money to buy a large skiff and try fishing. King salmon only sold for three cents a pound and a baker's dozen of large dungeness crab sold for one dollar and fifty cents but still they were able to earn money for steamship tickets on north to Juneau.

Gunnar spent his first years in town working for the water department. After he obtained his U.S. citizenship papers he joined the army. When his military service ended, he returned to Juneau and seriously pursued earning a living by fishing and trapping. After spending several years fishing and trapping in Funter Bay, Gunnar decided that he wanted to build a home there. Sam Pekovich, Sr., gave his permission to build on one of his mining claims.

and in 1948 Gunnar began a two-year project of clearing land and building a log home without benefit of power tools.

When I arrived as Gunnar's bride in 1958, I wondered what my new home would be like. Gunnar described it to me as "a little shack on the beach."

After getting Lauren situated in Juneau so that she could attend school there, I arrived in Funter Bay May 13 aboard Art Berthold's boat, the *Fern II*. It was a windy day, and the water was so choppy that Art decided to drop anchor and wait until the wind died down before rowing ashore. Gunnar had other ideas. He got into his sixteen-foot skiff, cranked up the small engine and scooted out to the *Fern II*. It didn't take him long to convince me that if he could make it out to us, he certainly could make it back to shore. I climbed aboard the skiff, grasped the seat with both hands, and away we went!

How pleasantly suprised I was to see a lovely log house surrounded by a beautiful yard complete with flagstone walkways. The living room was dominated by a huge flagstone fireplace. There also was a bedroom, a fully equipped bathroom, and a large kitchen, and the house was plumbed with running water and electricity through-out. Gunnar was ahead of the times; he had buried all the electricity wires in conduit from the generator shed to the house. I was beginning to learn that my husband was not only a very talented man, he was a perfectionist. When I entered the house, I was welcomed with a cozy, roaring fire in the fireplace, and soon had settled in for what were to be the most interesting, rewarding twenty-one years of my life.

Funter Bay is situated on the west side of Admiralty Island, about twenty miles from Juneau by boat. There is an old cannery site that can be seen on the northwest side upon entering the bay. The remains of the Alaska Admiralty Gold Mine were on the east side of the bay, south of Gunnar's cabin.

About six couples lived in the bay year-round. The first year or two I didn't visit the neighbors very much, as Gunnar did all the errands and picked up the mail delivered to the cannery site once a week. Even though neighbors did visit us from time to time, when work and weather permitted, I was lonely and missed my children. Lauren was living with friends in Juneau in order to attend school, and Gerald had joined the marines before I left California. Getting the mail once a week was always a big event. Don Gallagher delivered it from Juneau on his boat, the *Forrester*, which he later sold to Dave Reischel. Dave delivered our mail until Channel Flying began bringing it by plane. The excitement over getting the mail was always heightened by the fact that we never knew *what* we were getting. Often the wrong mail bag was left, and on one occasion every letter was covered with white paint where a gallon pail of paint had spilled inside the bag.

One of the first people I met at Funter Bay was Rodo Pekovich, caretaker of the buildings at the old Alaska Admiralty Gold Mine. Rodo had worked for the mine for some forty years and had been the company's mail carrier. After the mail was dropped off in Funter, Rodo carried it to the end of the mine road, then crossed 3,475-foot Mount Barron over the saddle of Admiralty Island to another mine at Hawk Inlet. He usually returned to Funter the same day. In those days there were no lightweight parkas or good insulated boots. Rodo disdained wool clothing and normally wore light clothes, such as jeans or overalls, and often wrapped his feet in pieces of burlap to keep them warm.

One day Rodo had to hike halfway up Mount Barron to retrieve a piece of equipment that weighed about fifty pounds. He returned to the mine site with the fifty-pound weight on his back, cleaned up, and then walked to our house for dinner, looking rested and relaxed. He was seventy years old.

Gunnar and I were inside the cabin when we heard three shots fired from the beach between our house and the old mine. This was a signal that meant someone needed help. From the house we could see Rodo sitting on a rock, and I ran to him while Gunnar put the skiff in the water and attached the motor to it. When I got to Rodo he was barely able to talk. Gunnar put him in the skiff and took him across the bay to Harold and Mary Hargraves's house so that they could call for an airplane over their radio-telephone hookup. Once the plane arrived, the pilot promised that he would see that Rodo got to Dr. Reiderer's office in Juneau. In town the pilot placed Rodo in a taxi, and the taxi driver let Rodo out at Dr. Reiderer's and drove away. Rodo was too weak to walk and had to crawl from the street to the doctor's office. Dr. Reiderer heard a scratching on the door and opened it to find a very sick Rodo lying on the steps. He rushed Rodo to the hospital, where the diagnosis was double pneumonia and tuberculosis.

We were just getting ready to celebrate Gunnar's birthday with all of our neighbors when Rodo returned home December 27 accompanied by a public health nurse. While I fixed their lunch, Gunnar and Harold Hargraves went over to Rodo's cabin to start a fire in his oil stove. I had been over earlier to tidy up the cabin and wash his bedding. Before leaving, the nurse asked that I check on Rodo to see that he took his eighteen pills each day. Gunnar volunteered to give Rodo his shot once a week. Rodo's friends in Juneau sent out a box of warm woolen clothes; it took a serious illness to change his mind, but he wore them. Each day I carried Rodo his evening meal and checked twice a day to see that he took his pills. We cared for Rodo this way for over a year, but once his health returned he was ready to climb mountains again.

Rodo had lived in Funter Bay nearly fifty years when he had to leave in 1971 to live with relatives in Juneau. On dark, moonless nights, friends and fishermen alike missed the lit kerosene lamp he kept in his window as a guide for fishermen wanting to tie up to the state dock.

Chilkoot Trail. Miners awaiting transportation on Dyea flats, 1897.

Chilkoot Trail, Dyea camp. Men, mules, and horses head out in 1898 across the flats near Dyea, Alaska, enroute to the Chilkoot pass and the gold-rich Yukon.

Marvel, Lazzette, Mae Carrol, and Clifford on the running board. Harry took them many times for a ride in his Model T Ford.

Lazzette standing in front of her mother (Marvel) and her grandmother, Mae Carrol, AKA "Esther" (right).

Tom Shearer, the tailor, the step-daughter, Lazzette.

Lazzette and Clifford in their Sunday best in Juneau.

Tom Shearer and Lazzette taking a break from work in the tailor shop.

Clifford, Lazzette, and neighbor, Virginia Kay, in front of the play log cabin the author's mother built.

Gunnar and Robert H. Horchover. Gunnar took great pride in his woodsheds. The Ohmans only burned wood that had seasoned four years for Lazzette's Monarch wood range. Gunnar cut the wood the perfect length for the fire box.

Lazzette with her grandmother in 1933. Jessie changed her name to "Mae" when she married Harry Carrol.

Gunnar and Lazzette Ohman, 1958.

Winter scene of Gunnar Ohman's cabin in Funter Bay. "Little shack on the beach!"

Gunnar and Keith Berggren (right) with a seventy-one pound red king salmon. Keith helped Gunnar during the peak of the season.

Gunnar was the chef when it came to preparing venison steaks in the fireplace. The fireplace was beautiful; it really produced the heat and delectable steaks. He burned only alderwood that had seasoned two years.

All hands helped prepare dinner while Lazzette took a break to take the weather observation and phone in to Juneau. Sylvia and Scott Horchover with Gunnar giving advice.

"Bell" and "Al" Schramen, Bess and Chet Kimmerly, from boats Aurora *and* Bess Chet, *with Lazzette in Funter Bay on the scow.*

Fern II. *Capt. Art Berthold leaving the scow in Pinta Cove after unloading supplies from Juneau, heading to Village Point to buy more fish.*

Rodo Pekovich, eighty-four years old in 1965, visiting for Sunday dinner.

Gunnar, Lazzette, and Lauren. Jerry stopped by while working for Fish & Game.

Big Boy—he was beautiful and terribly spoiled— checking his feed box.

Bambi the day we moved from the scow in late September, resting on the beach in front of her new "home."

Gunnar Ohman, fifty-eight years old, at his smokehouse at the end of the scow in Funter Bay. It was hard to beat his kippered salmon.

Fish Camp

Before I arrived at Funter, it had been Gunnar's habit to spend each summer at his fish camp, located a few miles south of Funter, in order to be closer to the fishing grounds. Gunnar returned to Funter just long enough to weed his garden and hoe the spuds, then off he went back to camp where he had fixed up an old abandoned cabin. During the summers of 1958 and 1959, when Lauren was home from school, the three of us lived at the camp. The original cabin was too small for all of us, so Gunnar built a second cabin and turned the original one over to Lauren. Eventually he added a workshed and sauna. While Gunnar was out fishing, Lauren and I had plenty of time to beachcomb, read, and get acquainted with our neighbors.

The first neighbor that we met was a female mink who had taken up residence under our cabin. Gunnar closed off her entrance when we realized that she was taking his old herring bait under the cabin and eating it there. Not long after this, the female mink was attacked and badly mauled by a male mink, and Gunnar felt terrible about closing off her only means of escape. He reopened the entrance, and from then on the female was our pet. Each day Lauren accompanied the female mink to the creek so that she could drink without fear of being attacked by the male. Whenever Lauren sat on the beach to read, the female mink curled up next to her for a nap. The mink also learned to watch for Gunnar to return from fishing, knowing that he would leave the bait herring in the skiff for her dinner.

She always came to our call whenever we had fish leftover from dinner.

Some of our other neighbors were not quite so sociable. A two-year-old bear was attracted to the smell of smoked salmon coming from Gunnar's small smokehouse that he had made from a barrel. After pounding on the top and sides, the bear finally gave up in frustration. We had other bears visit our garden each night and dig it up to get to the herring Gunnar buried there for fertilizer. Their visits became such a nuisance that Gunnar gave up fertilizing the garden in this manner.

An incident that I shall never forget occurred during the time that Lauren was away attending a church camp. I was awakened during the middle of the night by a loud, piercing scream. It scared me, and I woke Gunnar. He wasn't too concerned and told me to go back to sleep— probably thought I was dreaming. But I spent a restless night wondering what had made that terrible, eerie cry. Early the following morning, Gunnar got up to go fishing, but soon returned to the cabin explaining that he knew what I had heard. Gunnar had an outhaul line for his skiff attached to a tripod with a heavy counterweight. This tripod was firmly planted in the ground near our cabin, and it would have taken quite a force to move it. When Gunnar got to the beach, he found that something had ripped the tripod up and pulled it and the weight down to the beach. He figured that a whale had become tangled in the outhaul line, causing the whale to panic and make the noise that I heard. Only a whale could have ripped the tripod loose and pulled it down to the shoreline. I'll never forget that scream. It was so loud that I swore the folks in Funter Bay should have heard it.

During my first summer at fish camp, there was an earthquake at Lituya Bay that registered eight points on the Richter scale. Lituya is situated near Yakutat in the Gulf of Alaska. It's about the last protective bay before entering the outside waters. That day we noticed that the tide came in faster than usual and that the water was really disturbed, but we didn't find out the reason until Gunnar delivered his fish to the scow in Funter.

There were three trolling boats anchored in Lituya during the earthquake. A man and his young son were on one: The man tied his son to the boat's mast to keep him from being washed overboard; then he held on to the wheel. It was a hair-raising experience for both of them. Miraculously, they were the only ones who survived to describe what happened. They saw one of the boats simply disappear, and the third, the *Sunmore*, made a run out of the bay over the sandbar at the mouth of the bay. The boat had just reached the outside waters when it was hit by a large swell that actually devoured it. The husband and wife aboard were never found.

The quake generated a landslide in Lituya Bay that dumped trees, soil, rock, and ice at an estimated speed of 155 miles per hour. Some people were enjoying a day's outing picking wild strawberries on a point south of Lituya Bay when the quake broke off the point. These people also disappeared, never to be found.

I developed a real appreciation for the force of Mother Nature during these years of living in the wilderness. For the most part she was benevolent, but I knew she had a mean temper. During our second summer at camp, just before Lauren was to be picked up by the Presbyterian church vessel, the *Anna Jackman*, for a trip to their camp, a bad storm hit the area, dumping kelp on the beach that was two feet deep in places. Lauren was worried that this was going to ruin her chance of going to camp. The kelp was so deep and covered such a wide area that it was impossible to get the skiff over it and out to the *Anna Jackman* when it arrived. A fisherman in a skiff lent a hand, and with gaffs and fish knives, he and Gunnar began hacking at the mess from the outer edge while Lauren and I whacked away at kelp on the beach. It took us six hours, but by the time the *Anna Jackman* arrived we had cleared out enough of the kelp to get the skiff to the water.

We spent three summers living at fish camp. During August, Lauren and I would return to Funter in our sixteen-foot skiff to prepare Lauren for school in Juneau. After she departed on Alaska Coastal's *Grumman Goose,* I returned to camp and helped Gunnar clean up the area, put in the wood for next season, and close the cabins. We returned to Funter Bay in two skiffs, loaded with gear. On one such return a whale came up so close to my skiff that he splashed water in my face. I veered, the whale dove, and·Gunnar never saw a thing. He was already thinking about trapping season and was preoccupied looking for mink trails.

In the earlier years when Gunnar hand-trolled in the Funter Bay area, fish traps were still being used by the Hawk Inlet cannery. The traps were located close to shore, and men loaded the fish from the traps onto a power barge, then headed for the cannery, where the salmon were processed immediately. Gunnar says that he believes the fish were often handled better when caught in the traps than they are today by hand trollers. Sometimes trollers tend to leave their catch on the deck too long and wait to dress them when time permits. Today the fishermen are beginning to realize what Gunnar has long known, that many fish are wasted through poor care and mishandling.

Winters at Funter Bay

It was good to get home. Before leaving fish camp, I gave a large grocery order to Art Berthold, who owned the fish-buying scow and the packer, *Fern II*. Art arrived in Funter with our order soon after our return from fish camp, and we worked like beavers getting everything unloaded, put away, and under cover. It was a full day's work; then it took another three days for Art and Gunnar to deliver the rest of the supplies to Funter's other residents. Once we had our supplies stored, we treated ourselves with a sauna, a few schnapps, and steaks that Art brought, cooked in the fireplace. Art usually stayed in the bay a few days visiting friends. There was no rush—the fishing season was over! This was also the time that Gunnar and I took a break before settling down for winter. Sometimes we returned to Juneau with Art or flew to town a week or so later. We usually made these trips every fall and spring. It was our time to socialize and shop for incidentals that we might need. Our home away from home was always with Frank and Gudrun Olson. I had known Gudrun since I was a teenager, and they were the first couple Gunnar met when he arrived in Juneau in 1932. We normally had all of our shopping finished in four days, and by the fifth day Gunnar was restless and ready to head for home.

By now we were into early October—time to harvest our garden. It worked best if we could harvest the carrots on a dry day with a little wind. Gunnar pulled the carrots and topped them while I laid them out on canvas to dry. By the time we finished placing the carrots in their special boxes in the root cellar, we usually had enough to last the winter. At the end of harvest the root cellar was packed full of Swedish potatoes, rutabagas, turnips, and carrots. I had also put up a good supply of jams, jellies, and syrup made from the blueberries and red huckleberries that I picked in the bay. I made pickles and relishes from kelp.

Once the root cellar was stocked, it was time for Gunnar to get the year's supply of meat. He loaded up his skiff with supplies and returned to the fish camp for a few days of hunting. Gunnar never hunted near the house—thought it was bad luck. He always got his allotted four deer, which he corned, canned, and made into hamburger, stew meat, or jerky.

It took a lot of hard work to get ready for winter, but we survived it without much difficulty. Gunnar always made sure that we had a good supply of seasoned wood. The log house was equipped with a shower and electricity throughout; lights for our house and the adjacent buildings ran off a battery bank. Gunnar also had a heated shop where he kept all his well-oiled tools and razor-sharp saws. I soon learned to put anything I took back exactly where I found it. Gunnar was as good at working with wood as he was with metal. He made practically everything we used, down to hinges for the gates and drift pins for the log floats. He also had an artistic side. Our house was decorated with his oil paintings of wildlife, some done on pieces of bear bread, and his beautiful hand-carved boxes inlaid with ivory. All his guns were decorated with inlaid ivory on which he had created scrimshaw designs of bear or deer.

We did not spend completely isolated fall and winter seasons at Funter. Thanksgiving and Christmas were always spent with our Funter Bay neighbors. Sometimes we had Thanksgiving dinner at the home of the Hargraves. Rodo Pekovich was usually present; other guests often included Scotty Todd, Harvey Smith, and Cora and Curly Warnock. Dinner was early, as all of us had to go home by skiff and needed to leave before dark. Most of our neighbors in the bay came by boat, but we also had friends fly in from Juneau for this special occasion.

On Christmas Day, Gunnar decorated the tree while I decorated the house. When Lauren was home from school, she and I made all of our decorations from bottle caps and mussel and clam shells. We listened to Christmas music on the radio, had a late supper, and opened gifts at midnight. Sometimes we had Harvey Smith and Phil Emerson, bachelors who lived in the bay, in for dinner.

Our big social event was December 27, Gunnar's birthday. We normally had an open house for everyone in the bay. I spent the day before baking bread and dinner rolls, and our friends in town, Olav and Rosellen Lillegravan, sent out their "care" package with fresh produce, frozen turkey, cranberries, yams, and some "cheer" to keep everyone warm and in a holiday spirit. I also ordered a turkey from town, along with all the trimmings, and baked Gunnar an elaborate birthday cake for the occasion.

Everyone in the bay usually gathered at the Hargraves for dinner on New Year's Eve. We learned that when you live away from the city, it is best to create your own social life, and when weather permitted, we all got together to celebrate birthdays and holidays, and at times just got together for another dinner.

Sometimes during the fall and winter, fishermen would bring their boats into Funter seeking refuge. On these dark, moonless nights, when I saw a boat come into the bay, I would turn on the kitchen light and flip it three times. If the skipper answered back with his spotlight, I knew it was someone we knew, and they would probably be ashore later. It was always a treat to have these fishermen come ashore bringing news from Juneau.

Friends

During all the years we were at Funter Bay, I don't think Bob and Sylvia Horchover ever missed a summer coming from Juneau to visit; and they never came without a "care" package, always saying, "hope you don't have this," as they pointed to the fresh fruits, cantaloupes, melons, cucumbers, grapes, and bananas. One time they brought a pineapple, and I told Gunnar, "I'll just set it in the window to ripen." I was embarrassed to admit that I didn't know what to do with it, as I had never even eaten fresh pineapple.

When the Horchovers came, we alternated as to who would be guest and who would be host. Either they came ashore for dinner with us, or their kids acted as a taxi and took us to their boat, the *Sylvia J.*

Soon after I arrived in Funter, I heard that Al and Bell Schramen were fishing on their troller, the *Aurora*, and sent word for them to visit us. I had known both of them when I was growing up in Juneau and had gone to school with Al's sister. For years they came into the bay, always bringing some kind of a "treat," and they continue to be good friends today.

Tom and Teddy Dahlstrand and Jack and Peggy Roemer were friends that we met through correspondence. After reading an article that I had written, published in *Alaska Magazine* in 1969, they sent me a Swedish-American cookbook. It was such a wonderful book that I immediately wrote a thank-you letter. Instead of answering my thank-you note, they sent us another package! From this we started a correspondence that developed into a long friendship.

In September 1972, Gunnar and I flew to Juneau to meet Tom and Jack for the first time. I had arranged for them to charter a small boat, which we all boarded for our trip to Funter. When we dropped anchor in Funter, Tom and Jack were met by Harold Hargraves, who came out in his skiff with his rifle across his lap. Harold knew that Gunnar and I were away and, not realizing we were aboard, wanted to know who was snooping around our place. It was a surprising welcome for these Ohioans. Tom and Jack spent their days fishing and their evenings ashore with us. When they left they gave us a roll of stamps and said, "Just keep writing."

The following September, Tom and Jack brought their wives, along with Gudrun Olson, whom they had picked up on their stop in Juneau. This was a vacation that the Dahlstrands and the Roemers repeated every fall—sometimes bringing other relatives, friends, or some of their employees. They would charter one or two boats, depending on the size of the party. When they pulled their boat into the bay and we heard Tom call out over the loudspeaker, "Gunnar, shall I let the Old Crow fly?" we knew our friends from Ohio had arrived.

In the fall of 1968, Gunnar and I went to Seattle so that Gunnar could have surgery on his foot, and we also needed to help with Mom, who had cancer. Mom died January 8, and by the time we returned to Funter Bay, we had been gone five long months. It was Valentine's Day when I called Funter and told the Hargraves that we were coming home. It had been a hard winter, and we were a little concerned about getting through the deep snow to our house. I told Harold that we would buy snow shovels and dig our way through when we got there. When we arrived the following day, we were pleasantly surprised to see that all the men in Funter Bay had dug a trail from the beach all the way to the house. Gudrun prepared our supper before we left Juneau so that we could have a relaxing dinner while the cabin was warming up.

With the help of our neighbors, Gunnar and I were soon sitting in front of our fireplace enjoying a hot drink. The next day Gunnar fired up the sauna, and it sure felt good to be back in our warm and comfortable home among good friends.

Fish Scow

From 1961 through 1971, Gunnar and I spent six months of each year living on a fish scow and buying fish for Art Berthold. Our buying season lasted from the first of April until the first of October. The first year we lived on a dilapidated, moldy old scow that I swore would collapse like a cracker box every time a storm came up. I was so grateful when Gunnar started building a new scow the following year. By the time the project was finished, we had a new plywood building that provided us with living quarters, a small grocery store, and plenty of space for handling the fish. We also had an icehouse, and at one end of the scow there were drums of fuel for the trolling boats.

After the fishermen secured their boats, they pitched their fish onto the scow for Gunnar to sort and weigh. He called out the weight while I made up the fish slips for each fisherman. After the fish were all weighed and recorded, the fisherman picked out whatever supplies he needed, placed them on the counter, then I tallied up his grocery bill, paid him for the fish, and off he would sail, just in time for another boat to tie up.

Sometimes Art's wife, Jennie, came aboard the scow to help out. Whenever Art was ready to take the fish into town, Jennie and I made out our grocery lists. We usually had special orders for the fishermen—a special pair of gloves, hooks, or any other gear they might need. Sometimes we ordered a ham or turkey or "spirits" needed to celebrate a special occasion. We even took in the fishermen's bags of dirty laundry so that Art could drop them off in town. Another service we provided was our "outgoing" mail box. Time was precious, and the fishermen could not waste it running into town. We also kept a pretty good stock of pocket books so the fishermen could pick up a book for "harbor" days—days that were too stormy to fish. The most popular items that we sold were steaks flown in by Channel Flying.

Gunnar built a smokehouse on the scow, and after the fishermen sold their catch, it was a tradition to give each fisherman and his crew a free sample of the smoked salmon along with a complimentary beer or soda pop. When a fisherman came alongside the scow and said, "Gunnar, I've got my spuds on," it meant they were looking forward to some freshly smoked salmon, which they placed on top of their cooked spuds.

Gunnar and Art built a small float, which was brought along when we moved the scow into Pinta Cove. He also built a makeshift dam in a creek in the cove and laid eight hundred feet of plastic hose from the dam to the small float, which was anchored near shore, allowing the fishermen to bring their boats alongside the float and take on a supply of clear, fresh water. Gunnar set up a twenty-five-gallon barrel with a faucet, which provided us with plenty of running water in our living quarters for bathing and laundry.

Lauren worked with us the first two summers, which was a big help. We were a little cramped—extra groceries were kept on a shelf over her bed, and supplies of fish books under it. Lauren worked like a trooper. One day she was filling a bucket with seawater to scrub down the deck when she fell overboard. After she pulled herself back onto the deck, she figured as long as she was wet, she might as well go for a good swim and dived back in.

In the meantime, I got out the tub and began heating lots of water. A warm bath would feel good after a swim in southeast Alaska's fifty-four-degree water.

Not all of the fishermen who did business with us were men. Myrl Flemming fished from her twenty-foot cruiser, *Flamingo*. Many times, when we were especially busy, Mryl pitched in to help. She made sure we had lots of fresh coffee to go with our hastily eaten doughnuts knowing that we didn't have time to stop for a real meal. Of course, there were days when Myrl was so tired she fell asleep on Lauren's cot while waiting for the coffee to perk.

Two other fisherwomen, Sherry Tuttle and Betty Castino, whom we really enjoyed, came up each summer from Tiburon, California, where they had jobs as physical education teachers. During the day they fished from a small cruiser but camped on shore on the beach across from the scow each night. Charles Eckhardt was on his troller, *Ukum*, near Mud Bay when he got his arm tangled in his gurdy while pulling in fish. The teachers heard his distress call on the radio and rushed to his assistance. Fortunately, the pilot of a Channel Flying floatplane also heard the call and was able to land and take Charles into Juneau for medical help. It wasn't safe to leave the large troller where Charlie had left it; so the girls brought it to the scow where it could be safely secured. They were pretty excited because it was their first time to handle a troller, but they did a great job.

We were grateful for marine radios, well-stocked first aid kits, and friends who were always willing to help out during an emergency. One such emergency happened when Art and his nephew, Duke Davis, were alongside the scow with the *Fern II*. Gunnar slipped on the floor in the fish house and landed on a fishbox, breaking two ribs. Gunnar was too much of a stubborn Swede to go into

Juneau for medical help and borrowed an elastic bandage from one of the fishermen to wear around his chest. We were very grateful that Duke decided not to leave with Art on the *Fern II*. I had never seen Gunnar in so much pain, and it was a relief to have Duke stay on for a few more days to help with the work.

Dr. Reiderer had helped me put together a first aid kit during one of my trips to Juneau and had given me some pointers in first aid. I got to be pretty good at taking fish hooks out of hands, treating fish poisoning, and doctoring an assortment of cuts and gashes.

During all the years that we worked and lived on the fish scow, I never got over being seasick during the rough weather. We always expected a pretty good storm to move in from the north during the last week of August, but one year it was worse than usual. I was resting in the scow, trying to combat seasickness, and happened to look out our window when a large swell hit our scow broadside. I could see that the scow was being turned end for end and knew that the wave must have broken our six-hundred-pound anchor chain. Gunnar poked his head through the door and told me to dress warmly in case the scow hit the beach and we had to jump off. After I dressed, I grabbed a flight bag and stuffed it with the money, mail, matches, some candy bars, and a bottle of Old Crow. In the meantime, Ned Albright came around Point Adolphous in his boat, *Omney*, and headed in our direction. Ned's boat was twenty-five feet long, and the scow was eighty feet, so there wasn't a lot Ned could do other than call for help from the *Fern II* and stand by in case we needed assistance. In the meantime, a twenty-five-foot boat pulled alongside the scow seeking protection. The skipper hollered to Gunnar over the noise of the wind and swells crashing over the scow that he wanted to tie up to us. Gunnar yelled back, "No way, your boat will bounce on top of our deck and be broken up!" The skipper said they were out of food, so I quickly threw some butterhorns into a sack and tossed it, along with a quart of milk, over to him. Gunnar secured a long line to a cleat on the scow, threw the line to the skipper, and the small boat laid off the end of the scow at a safe distance until the storm let up. It took Art and Jennie about two hours to arrive on the *Fern II*. Before the storm, I had baked a strawberry shortcake to give Art and Jennie, knowing that they would be in later that evening. I don't know how I did it, or why, but when the *Fern II* pulled alongside the boat during the storm, I somehow tossed that cake over to Art. Waves were crashing clear over the top of the scow, but somehow our two other anchors held and kept us off the beach.

In the summer of 1967, we had the scow in Funter Bay when a large yacht pulled alongside. Lee and Myrtle Chambers had sailed their boat, *Blackfish*, up from Seattle. They came to the scow hoping to buy cigarettes. Gunnar had just finished cooking a batch of Dungeness crab and handed Myrtle a fresh cooked crab as soon as she stepped off the boat. That gesture was the beginning of a long friendship. The year that Gunnar and I were in Seattle, just before Mom died, Lee and Myrtle took us aboard the *Blackfish* for a sail from Lake Union. We sailed through the locks to the open sea, which was a new and fascinating experience for me. At the end of the evening we docked at Ivar's restaurant—just stepped off the boat and walked directly into the restaurant. It may not have compared to being handed a fresh cooked crab as soon as you stepped off the boat, but it was a surprise and a perfect way to end a wonderful day and evening.

The ten years that we lived on the scow were hard work, and we were always grateful for the end of fishing season so that we could return to Funter Bay. But we met people that we will never forget.

Wildlife

Some of the most poignant and amusing memories during those years we lived in Funter Bay, the fish camp, and on the fish scow, were provided by some of the most intelligent, cunning, and ornery critters you could ever meet.

American bald eagles are as common a sight in southeast Alaska as the ravens and crows, and Gunnar still laughs at the time I got into a tug of war match with one of these stoic looking national birds. It was winter, and I had developed a strong hunger for crab, when one morning I saw an eagle dig up a crab from the beach. I put on my boots, ran down to the beach, and grabbed that crab right out of the eagle's beak! He scowled at me with that blinking eagle stare, but he was too shocked to move. I was so hungry for cooked crab that I didn't even consider the pain that eagle could have inflicted with his sharp claws. Boy, did that cooked crab taste good!

Between me and the ravens, the eagles certainly had a rough time of it. I've seen ravens harass eagles in flight— sometimes to keep the eagles from the raven nests, but other times it seemed to be just for the orneriness of it. On the ground the ravens really take advantage of the eagle's clumsy, slow movements. One winter day I watched two ravens team up to steal a fish that an eagle had found on the beach. Just as the eagle was about to settle down for a quiet dinner, the ravens landed—one near the eagle's tail and the other near its wing. All of a sudden the larger raven grabbed the eagle's wing and pulled it full length, while the other raven pulled on his tail. They kept this routine up until the eagle finally became so frustrated that he flew away, leaving his dinner behind for the ravens.

Another time we watched an eagle try to catch a duck for dinner. Every time the duck came up for air, the eagle was right on top of him, forcing the duck to dive again. The eagle kept his attack up until the duck was nearly exhausted. Fortunately for the duck, a seagull and some crows showed up and pestered the eagle until he flew off. With that kind of luck, I wondered how so many eagles survived the winter.

Although the crows often were very protective of one another, they also had terribly brutal fights, usually fighting until one was killed. During one fight that I witnessed, it seemed that the entire rookery was gathered around the two combatants, yelling and making a terrible racket. It was something to watch; it reminded me of ringside at a boxing match.

Later Gunnar and I saw something we could hardly believe. That day Gunnar and I again heard the crows making a racket. We looked outside and saw that they were all gathered around a crow that we had nicknamed Club Foot. At first I thought it was a fight between Club Foot and another crow, but as we continued watching, it appeared that Club Foot was injured. A crow got under each of Club Foot's wings, and the two took off with the injured bird between them, heading across the bay toward the trees where they roosted. It puzzled me to see how protective and helpful they could be to one another, yet never take sides or interfere during a fight.

An unusual incident that we heard about from Ned Albright concerned his encounter with a humpback whale. Ned was fishing off his troller, and Ted and Doris Samples were on their boat, the *Diver*, when a whale dove under their boats and reappeared in front of the *Omney's* bow, causing Ned to hurriedly kick the *Omney* into reverse to avoid a collision. This happened several times until Ned veered off and headed toward a buyer's fish scow. Then the whale turned its attention toward the *Diver*, giving it the same attention. By the time the *Diver* reached the scow, poor Doris was white as a sheet and scared to death. This was really unusual behavior for a whale, and no one could figure out what had attracted it or what its motivation was.

We never lacked for pets on the fish scow or at our home in Funter. Our first year on the scow, a pair of martin swallows built their nest over our doors inside the scow. The second year we had a new scow and wondered if the swallows would return. They did, and again built their nest over the doors. By July 5, the female had laid three eggs. It was necessary for us to tow the scow from Funter to Pinta Cove, and Gunnar made sure that the swallows were inside the scow before we got underway. Between seven and nine hours later we were at Pinta Cove, and when Gunnar opened the doors, the two swallows flew off searching for food, but soon returned. Eventually Gunnar had these swallows trained to stay on the side of the scow where he had water and could keep the deck washed.

The female swallow returned to our scow every summer, but not with the same mate. In fact, her first mate was no family man; he wouldn't help her with the offspring and required constant nagging. The last time I saw him, he had just endured a terrible scolding, had a look on his face as if to say, "To hell with this," and took off. He never returned, and it was impossible for the female to feed the five babies alone. She quickly struck each chick on the back of the head, instantly killing it. Although the female returned to our scow for several years, she never used that nest again, but built another nest over a door on the opposite side of the scow. This was the first time that we saw her mates refuse to carry their share of the burden with their offspring.

Sometimes, particularly on rainy days, our swallows would fly down to the grocery counter, sit there and "talk" to us. One day I was busy totaling up a fisherman's catch, making out his fish slip, and getting his money while he waited on the other side of the counter.

"I see you have your swallows back," he said. "Yes, we have," I replied, not bothering to look up while I continued totaling up the fish slip. When I finally looked at him, I was shocked to see that one of the swallows had dropped excrement right down on the middle of the man's forehead, and it ran down the length of his nose! I hastily mumbled, "I'm sorry. Excuse me," retreated to the apartment and doubled over laughing. As soon as I got control of myself, I returned to the counter, finished waiting on the fishermen (who had cleaned his face with his sleeve), and silently gave thanks that this fishermen had a sense of humor.

The next thing that Gunnar taught the swallows was to stay away from the store area.

At the end of one fishing season we had just returned to Funter Bay, and as we pulled up to the state float, I heard a deer call. I looked toward the beach, and there it was—a "Bambi." I called to it, and the fawn swam to the float. Gunnar reached down and pulled the deer up onto the float. When Gunnar sat down on a bench, the "Bambi" readily jumped on his lap. The fawn had been found by some loggers who were working in Funter. They had a female golden retriever that adopted Bambi and cared for it as though it were a pup. At first the loggers fed Bambi with a baby bottle until she was large enough to eat dog food. By the time we arrived, she had eaten all the dog food and was getting pretty hungry and thin.

Since fishermen were still coming into the bay to sell their catch, we continued living on the scow for a few days. Each evening, Gunnar put Bambi into his skiff and rowed her to shore to spend the night and returned to shore the following morning to bring her back to the scow. One night it was too stormy to row Bambi back to shore, so we put her in the fish house for the night. Lord! What an evening! Deer are related to the goat family, and Bambi was no exception. All night long she climbed over the blockades, peeked through the keyhole, and cried and cried. I was never so glad to see morning.

As soon as fishing season closed, Gunnar and Art pushed the scow up on shore at high tide. When I walked up to the house, Bambi followed along like a well-trained pup. That fall we had to teach Bambi to eat her own natural foods. Gunnar took her into the woods and introduced her to eating gray moss that grew on the trees, and Bambi took to the moss like a baby takes to candy. Sometimes Gunnar stuffed some moss inside his shirt to feed her at home. Bambi would stand on her hind legs, gently place her two front hoofs on Gunnar's shoulders and beg for more moss.

She loved to play. If I was in the yard and bent down to help Gunnar with something, Bambi would grab me by the hair—her signal that she wanted to play. That fall we decided not to make our annual trip into town because we were reluctant to leave Bambi until she could feed herself. I placed a rug on our front porch where Bambi often slept during the day. Each night she bedded somewhere in the nearby woods.

One day we were having lunch when Bambi jumped up on the porch. All of a sudden Gunnar jumped up, ran out the door, grabbed the broom, and butted Bambi off the porch, saying, "Don't you ever pee on this porch again!" From that day on Bambi was housebroken.

When Bambi was a year and a half old, we decided that we could take our fall trip into town. Bambi was well on her way to living her own life, and we looked forward to seeing the twins that she would likely have in the spring. Before we left, Gunnar had warned a hunter in the area that "if a deer runs up to you, don't shoot, It's a pet." On the day we left, Bambi met this man on the mine road and happily ran up to him. Greedy for easy meat, the hunter shot Bambi.

There were other deer that we fed during the winter months. We never fed them during hunting season, though, as we did not want to encourage them to go near people at that time. The deer seemed to sense when hunting season was over because at the end of December we would see them popping out all along the beach, looking toward our house. When the snow got so deep that the deer had a hard time finding feed, we put out oats, vegetable peelings, and fruit scraps.

Big Boy was a large buck that we fed for nearly twenty years. He was big, beautiful, and very selfish when it came to sharing food. One time Big Boy disappeared for two years. I was sure he had been shot. All of a sudden, he reappeared on our back porch with his head in an empty oat bucket. Funter Bay's deer were pretty well-fed during the winter, as all of the people in the bay ordered fifty-pound bags of oats to feed them.

We also had a family of land otters in the bay. The adult otters generally kept their young in the woods, near a pond. Once the pups were old enough, mama and papa otter brought them down the creek, playing with them all the while. Sometimes a pup got separated from its parent, and l would go down to the beach and give a sharp whistle. Curious about the whistle, the pup would raise out of the water and come toward me. As long as I kept whistling, the pup would come until it was close enough to see that I wasn't its mama, then it would take off crying. Once the pups became used to me, they would swim alongside the shoreline while I walked along the edge of the water. I talked to them all the time, and they seemed to enjoy my presence.

One time when Gunnar and I were about to board a Channel Flying airplane for a trip to Juneau, all six of the otters swam out to the float, each one carrying a fish in its mouth. When the pilot asked, "What's this?" I explained that the otters considered the float their dining table. All the while we loaded the plane, the otters ate their meal and played, seemingly totally oblivious to our presence.

Observing the wild animals in Funter Bay was better than watching any movie or television show.

Conclusion

In the fall of 1973, a new element was added to my daily routine at Funter. Personnel from the National Weather Service arrived in a chartered plane to ask if I would consider being a weather observer. After I agreed to do it, I had to study a manual sent out by the National Oceanic Administration in preparation for a test that I was to take in the spring. I passed the test, missing only one out of a hundred questions. The weather service, all of the necessary equipment, and a crew to install it came by a chartered boat, and a large antenna was sent over by helicopter. I made eight weather observations a day—sometimes more, depending on the weather. After writing up my reports, I called them in to the weather service over a special radio-telephone and once a month sent a copy of my report to the weather office in Anchorage and to the main office in Maryland. I could never resist adding a personal note to these reports, such as observing the migration of swans, cranes, or geese, or reporting the activities of the bear, deer, or otter that I had seen that day. There was just too much happening in Funter Bay to limit my reports to numbers and measures.

In the summer of 1978, Gunnar was replacing a line that was attached to our counterweighted stairway to the attic. To reach the line, Gunnar had to place the ladder on top of a box. While Gunnar was working, the box gave way and Gunnar fell, hitting his head on the pantry door. Gunnar took it easy the rest of the day, but by evening was complaining that his eyes were not right. Ironically, the Dahlstrands from Ohio arrived aboard a charter boat that evening and had a friend with them who was an eye specialist. After checking Gunnar's eyes, he decided to call Dr. Page in Juneau, as he suspected that Gunnar had a detached retina. Gunnar left with them early the following morning. Dr. Page confirmed the specialist's diagnosis, but decided against surgery, as Gunnar also was suffering from hardening of the arteries.

After Gunnar returned to Funter, we soon realized that continuing to live in a remote area would be very difficult—we would be too dependent on our friends. There were so many chores, such as chopping wood, that Gunnar could no longer do for fear of damaging the retina in his other eye. It was a heart-wrenching decision, but we decided to move to Juneau.

Dr. Robert Horchover and his family took all of our supplies out of our root cellar and carried them to Juneau where Gudrun stored them until we were settled. Paul Johnson brought his fishing boat, *Nova*, to pick up the rest of our things, and by November 1, 1979, Gunnar and I were ready to leave. Today we live in a comfortable house in downtown Juneau, and I am grateful that we are able to visit most of the good friends that we made while we lived in Funter Bay.

The happiest days of my life were spent with Gunnar at his little shack on the beach in Funter Bay.

A pleasant part of living in Juneau is attending meetings of the Pioneers of Alaska. Am I an Alaskan pioneer? I was born and grew up in southeast Alaska, spent all of my life in Alaska, except for the brief time I spent in California, so I guess that makes me a pioneer. Certainly my grandparents were pioneers.

Many other Alaskans have done and seen the things I have, but I do believe that I have lived a life-style that is quickly disappearing in Alaska and in many cases has already disappeared. There are no more dairy farms in Juneau (one was practically in downtown Juneau) and the gold mines have disappeared, along with the fox farms that once populated nearly every island in southeast Alaska. The beautiful log cabin that Gunnar so lovingly built is now part of a lodge that caters to tourists who come to Alaska seeking a "wilderness experience."

I hope that what I have told here will not only give my children and grandchildren some knowledge of their grandparents and what their lives were like, but will also provide the reader with an appreciation of what it was like living in Gunnar's "little shack on the beach" in Funter Bay.